Fresh from the Brain

Georgina Spoors

BookLeaf
Publishing
India | USA | UK

Presentation by *BookLeaf Publishing*

Web: www.bookleafpub.com

E-mail: info@bookleafpub.com

ISBN: 9789357446778

First edition 2022

Knees

Sun roasting
Backs warm
The smell of onions cooking
To the beat of a funky baseline
And soulful vocal notes

A slow morning
Sleepy and warm
Never far from a hand to hold
Or a body to lie with

Peace. Waves. A child excited about the sand,
wanting to say hello

Bleeding feet and a new t-shirt
Summer has been given a new lease

Back to it

Back again
With fresher eyes
Seeing more and being thankful for what
I overlooked
Time without pressure
Without constantly anticipating the next thing
Free time
As it should be
Spent in 2s and 3s
like it should be,
at my age

In Memory of the Yellow Bicycle of Dreams

There she was again
To brighten my day
The girl with the yellow bicycle

Posture perfect
Pedals turned effortlessly
In straight-legged jeans

She leans into the corner - left -
And flies down the road
While the wind practices plaiting her hair

It's as if she holds the world
At the tips of her fingers,
serene smile passing no judgement.

The promenade seems made
Especially for her
The sea greets her,
Then bows and gently recedes

Even the grey of the sky
Is no match for the sunshine
She holds in the frame beneath her.

Each time that I see her,
I can't help but smile
At the girl with the yellow bicycle.

Twenty Eight

I guess this is what you'd call a 'bad day'
It is full of cloud, inside and out
It is the kind of warm that is suffocating
My clothes don't feel right
The trousers are too tight around my ankles.
If I had a giant eraser, I would take the lips from
my face so I had an excuse not to participate in
conversation
I might go too far and erase myself completely -
It is better that I don't have it.
Instead I lie every which way and try to dissolve
I try to sink; I feel heavy enough to go right
through the floor
But here I am. Balancing precariously on the
Earth
Feeling its slow turn today more than usual
And turn it does
Even as I am motionless
Lead in my bones and my brain
Full of nothing much, empty
but unable to carry more

Cats Can See the Wind

Cats can see the wind
That's what my granny always says
They sit there, seeing the world move in ways
we cannot
Well today, even I can see the wind
It's trying to tear the trees from the earth
Their usual twirling dance has become raucous
and wild, and they bend further than their trunks
are accustomed to

Sea spray fills the air, the whole place feels alive
Frenetic
It is one of those days where the power of the
earth is undeniable, you feel small and
powerless in its unforgiving hold.
It screams and rips through the doors and the
windows,
Humans small and safe inside the walls
Only to be blown away once they step one foot
outside

Mind Reading?

People don't really pay attention
Do you usually wear a skirt? Or trousers?
It has been 5months
No-one asks where your bruise came from
Or why your eyes are red
They are too busy in their own heads
Planning and worrying and wondering and creating
No-one really sees

So why do u expect them to read your mind?

Are you okay?

I won't cry, no
I will be quiet
I will feel so deeply that all I emit is a strange,
cold, discomfort
You won't speak to me
I will just stand and do what I'm told to
Grit my teeth
Turmoil on the inside
Eerie stillness on the outside
You stand there like prey recognising danger
I am the predatory stillness before the pounce
You stand paralysed, tensed, until the danger has
passed
Or so you thought.
Snap. Too late. It got you.

Side Glances

A strange thing, attraction
Caught in someone's step
In their smile
In the way they speak
Or just the way they fill their own space, the
way they go about existing
Excitement over small things
A new look
A pet name
An extra 'x' on the last line
So much riding on a simple reply

Please

We dance, with knives in our belts and flowers
in our hair
Catch me if you can... (please)

Fine Wine

A hazy day
Half here half not
Melancholy happiness
Heart full
I think

Bottle it
To have a sip later
When real life comes back
Keep me going til the next time

Keats

Keats
100 years
But barely older than I am
Daisies growing over him
Peaceful

I grow no daisies.

The earth is not good enough just yet
Maybe that's for the best
I enjoy the feeling of sunshine
Without looking through petals
I do not want their dappled shade
Let me burn so I know I'm here
Right here
Now.

Hollow Legs

A slice of different lives
Some savoured on the tongue
Some discarded after one bite
Some devoured
Some eaten daintily with a tiny fork
I will try them all until I find one that fills me up

To my Little Onion

In this card I enclose...

A snippet of the tune that a man walked past
whistling
The warmth provided by the sun on my legs
A cheer of pure unadulterated joy given at the
sight of a sign saying 'fresh local milk'
The addictive silkiness of the furry jacket we all
stopped to stroke in M&S
The lovely tingle of the ginger shot we drank
together (and immediately regretted)

... and it's not even midday!

Standing is Best

THREE
TWO
ONE

The place erupts
The euphoria of collective feeling
Bodies moving; freed of all burden
Driven by the need to BE
To be here
To be felt
To be a part of something

JUMP
JUMP
JUMP

Cups fly through the air
Insecurity abandoned
We are lost to ourselves
And it doesn't matter
We are here
We are felt
We are a part of something

First Note

Hair on end
Skin prickling
Smiles spreading,
infectious

Bass rumbles
Chests heave
Hands reach out
Connecting

The Kick hits
Feet tingle
Knees bent
Preparing

Split second
Lights flash
Band screams
We're JUMPING

Concert

Fingers reach outwards
Extending the emotion
And it grows and grows

Oh.

Unjustified hurt
A sense of inbalance
Power has shifted
You're wearing my trousers.
I'm wearing your shirt.
How long did you know
How long did you wait
Were your words rehearsed -
Pre-planned with your mates?
Awkwardness sits
Where warmth used to be
You seem funnier now,
Perfect words against my clumsy ones.
I feel separate from you
Though I pushed you away
And now you've stood - the 'bigger man' -
I sort of want you to stay.

Refresh the Feed

Wind howling
Chocolate for breakfast
Only one 7 o'clock in the day
Sunny outside, people indoors
Another 700 deaths today.
That makes over 10,000
In the UK alone
The earth is shouting at us - I can't say I blame her.
No pasta, no flour , no loo roll, no soap.
2 metres apart at all times.
At least everyone knows how to wash their hands now.

Companies are collapsing,
Grandparents 'zooming' around
The dolphins are back in Italy
And goats have taken over Wales.
I heard today
That in Spain they're 'dog walking' stuffed animals
It turns out people can be quite creative
When they've exhausted Instagram by 11am